G000153525

Chinese Astrology

Chinese Astrology

ARIEL BOOKS

**Andrews McMeel
Publishing**

Kansas City

A GUIDE TO THE SIGNS

Julie Mars

Chinese astrological signs
illustrated by Kristen Balouch

Illustrations of Chinese astrological signs
copyright © by Kristen Balouch

ISBN: 0-7407-0061-8
Library of Congress Catalog Card Number:
99-60616

Contents

A Brief History of Chinese Astrology

Once upon a time, the dying Buddha, wishing to gaze upon his animal friends, prepared a feast and invited all the creatures of Earth to attend. But only twelve animals came: the Rat, the Ox, the Tiger, the Rabbit, the Dragon, the Snake, the Horse, the Sheep, the Monkey, the Rooster, the Dog, and the Pig. To show his appreciation, Buddha honored each animal with a year of its own, to be

repeated in a twelve-year cycle—forever after.

So goes the legend behind Chinese astrology, a system based on the lunar calendar. For centuries, Chinese astrology remained a closely guarded secret. Today, people from all around the world eagerly study Chinese astrology in order to understand the mysterious human personality.

To become familiar with the symbolism of the twelve Chinese animals is to enter a world of magic, mystery, and old-fashioned common sense. But first, the basics.

Understanding
Chinese Astrology

Not only are animals assigned to years in Chinese astrology, they are also assigned to hours of the day: The Chinese day is divided into twelve two-hour periods. Your birth-year animal describes your essential character; your birth-hour animal shows how you are viewed by others—and how you present yourself to the world.

Students of Chinese astrology must also become familiar with the important concepts of Yin and Yang, as well as the Five Elements—because each hour, each day, and each year are a combination of animal power, element, and Yin/Yang qualities.

YIN AND YANG

Chinese astrologers believe that all the powers of Earth are balanced by two kinds of energy: Yin, feminine and negative; and Yang, masculine and positive. Yin symbolizes receptivity, passivity, and rest and is associated with the Moon, night, water, sweetness, and emotion.

Yang symbolizes action, energy, and movement. It is associated with the Sun, daylight, fire, impermeability, and drive.

In order to achieve harmony and peaceful growth, these two forces must balance each other. Yin and Yang years alternate and complement each other. There are six Yin animals—Ox, Rabbit, Snake, Sheep, Rooster, and Pig. The six Yang animals are Rat, Tiger, Dragon, Horse, Monkey, and Dog.

THE FIVE ELEMENTS
In the Chinese system, all matter is

divided into Five Elements (or modifiers). These elements influence—and even change—one's personality. They are Wood, which ignites the powers of imagination; Fire, related to passion and energy; Earth, inspiring stability and practicality; Metal, which helps create strong will; and Water, which leads to sensitivity and tact.

The Five Elements are also linked to the five planets known to the Chinese at that time: Wood with Jupiter; Fire with Mars; Earth with Saturn; Metal with Venus; and Water with Mercury. Each element extends its influence over two years—one Yin and one Yang—in addition to two hours in each twenty-four-hour period.

THE SYSTEM

A full cycle of animal, element, and Yin-Yang polarity is completed every sixty years. Each cycle begins with the Wood Rat and ends with the Water Pig. Our present cycle began in 1984 and will end in the year 2044. Consult the chart beginning on page 88 to find your Chinese astrological sign.

THE RAT

Sociable, intelligent, and group-oriented, Rats are often found at the very center of the group. Agile and quick, they're admired for their intuition and passion—and sex appeal. Their ability to view situations from several perspectives at once—a feat of intellectual gymnastics—is truly impressive.

Rats typically love risk, and others marvel at the Rat's combination of self-control and willingness to take a chance. A gamble is often a sure thing in the Rat's powerful paws!

ALL ABOUT THE RAT

Chinese Name: SHU

Hours of Day: 11:00 P.M. to 12:59 A.M.

Month: December

Natural Friends: Monkeys and Dragons

Best to Avoid: Horses

Color: Blue

Occupations: Communications, research, management

Gems: Diamonds and Amethysts

Lucky Numbers: 1, 10, 11, 14, 41, 45

Famous Rats: Lauren Bacall, Mata Hari, Buddy Holly, Gene Kelly, Wolfgang Amadeus Mozart, William Shakespeare

THE OX

Hard-working, dependable, and predictable are words associated with the Ox. Steady and determined to finish the job, Oxen are valued in both the workplace and the home. Their endurance and integrity often earn them positions of trust.

Because typical Oxen prefer familiar pastures, few are tempted to pursue an adventurous or spontaneous lifestyle. Through careful and methodical saving, Oxen usually live in comfort their whole lives. They tend to be deeply sensual—and their passion is built to last!

ALL ABOUT THE OX

Chinese Name: NIU

Hours of Day: 1:00 A.M. to 2:59 A.M.

Month: January

Natural Friends: Roosters and Snakes

Best to Avoid: Sheep

Color: Violet

Occupations: Design and building, excavation, physical therapy

Gems: Emeralds and Jade

Lucky Numbers: 1, 12, 15, 33, 51, 53

Famous Oxen: Napoléon Bonaparte, Jackie Collins, Walt Disney, George Gershwin, Meryl Streep, Margaret Thatcher

THE TIGER

Tigers are sleek, powerful, freedom-loving, and restless. They're forever on the prowl—in search of new challenges, action, and passionate attachments.

Tigers are admired for their courage, magnetism, and intensity . . . but sometimes criticized for their impulsiveness, their bossiness, and their mighty (and intimidating) roar. They tend to act first and think later, which leads first to regret, but ultimately to wisdom and self-control. Tigers add a touch of class—and sexiness—to their surroundings.

ALL ABOUT THE TIGER

Chinese Name: HU

Hours of Day: 3:00 A.M. to 4:59 A.M.

Month: February

Natural Friends: Horses and Dogs

Best to Avoid: Monkeys

Color: Green

Occupations: Art, politics, performance

Gems: Rubies and Diamonds

Lucky Numbers: 4, 5, 7, 9, 45, 54

Famous Tigers: Ludwig van Beethoven, Agatha Christie, Marie Curie, Charles de Gaulle, Groucho Marx, Karl Marx, Demi Moore

THE RABBIT *(sometimes called the Cat)*

Gentle, artistic, and diplomatic, Rabbits are extremely sensitive. A harsh word or a cold look might send them scurrying. This tendency leads to a personality that is both tactful and wise.

Because Rabbits are insightful, they are often able to solve complex problems. A natural respect for others builds a strong foundation for friendship, but when it comes to love, Rabbits require sensitivity—and provide the surprises that keep romance thriving.

ALL ABOUT THE RABBIT

Chinese Name: TU

Hours of Day: 5:00 A.M. to 6:59 A.M.

Month: March

Natural Friends: Sheep and Pigs

Best to Avoid: Roosters

Color: Light Green

Occupations: Health care, teaching, law

Gems: Pearls and Emeralds

Lucky Numbers: 1, 3, 5, 15, 19, 35

Famous Rabbits: Billie Holiday, Rudolf
Nureyev, Eva Perón, Queen Victoria,
Andy Warhol, Orson Welles

THE DRAGON

The fire-breathing Dragon makes demands and requires constant attention. Larger than life, Dragons tend to be magnetic and decisive . . . but brutally frank. They may exhibit egotistical tendencies—and heaven help those who dare to point out their flaws!

They often devote themselves to idealistic pursuits. Dragons strive for perfection in themselves and expect it from others, but most Dragons have a soft, sentimental underbelly. They'll willingly leap into love—and they need tenderness forever after.

ALL ABOUT THE DRAGON

Chinese Name: LONG

Hours of Day: 7:00 A.M. to 8:59 A.M.

Month: April

Natural Friends: Rats and Monkeys

Best to Avoid: Dogs

Color: Blue-green

Occupations: Computer programming, advertising, sales

Gems: Sapphires and Opals

Lucky Numbers: 3, 4, 24, 35, 36, 45

Famous Dragons: Joan of Arc, Che Guevara, Martin Luther King Jr., Florence Nightingale, Pele, Ringo Starr

THE SNAKE

The Snake is the symbol of wisdom. Calm and silent, it easily sheds its skin—old identities. This ability to adapt and change is the Snake's key trait.

Snakes may be mistrustful and slow to enter into intimate relationships. They are frequently accused of being secretive and possessive—and it's usually true. Great readers and thinkers, Snakes are typically resourceful, shrewd, and philosophical. Snakes are legendary in their sensuality and usually possess a healthy, strong sex drive.

ALL ABOUT THE SNAKE

Chinese Name: SHE

Hours of Day: 9:00 A.M. to 10:59 A.M.

Month: May

Natural Friends: Oxen and Roosters

Best to Avoid: Pigs

Color: Red

Occupations: Mental health care, philosophy, surgery

Gems: Bloodstone and Topaz

Lucky Numbers: 1, 2, 4, 24, 42, 46

Famous Snakes: Charles Darwin, Bob Dylan, Mahatma Gandhi, Greta Garbo, Abraham Lincoln, Jackie Kennedy Onassis, Mae West

THE HORSE

Free-spirited Horses tend to consider the world their home and everyone in it their friend. They are typically smart, energetic, strong willed, and driven to lead. Admired for their gift of gab, Horses are sociable and typically prefer to run with a herd.

Because they tend to be easily bored, Horses need variety to spice up their lives. And the spicier, the better! They may travel the world, change jobs with alarming frequency, and live only for the moment. In love, Horses must learn compromise—a task that requires practice.

ALL ABOUT THE HORSE

Chinese Name: MA

Hours of Day: 11:00 A.M. to 12:59 P.M.

Month: June

Natural Friends: Tigers and Dogs

Best to Avoid: Rats

Color: Orange

Occupations: Travel professions, diplomacy, journalism

Gems: Turquoise and Topaz

Lucky Numbers: 1, 3, 4, 8, 13, 14

Famous Horses: Muhammad Ali, Clint Eastwood, Billy Graham, Rita Hayworth, Genghis Khan, Barbra Streisand, Boris Yeltsin

THE SHEEP *(sometimes called the Goat)*

The Sheep is perhaps the most compassionate of all the animals. This concern for others results in a softness that is sometimes mistaken for fragility. But Sheep are stable, determined, and diplomatic. Their extreme sensitivity is a secret source of strength.

They're not known for practicality, but their tact and good manners more than compensate for the occasional lapses into dreamy idealism. In romance, Sheep demand the real thing: security, passion, and complete commitment.

ALL ABOUT THE SHEEP

Chinese Name: YANG

Hours of Day: 1:00 P.M. to 2:59 P.M.

Month: July

Natural Friends: Rabbits and Pigs

Best to Avoid: Oxen

Colors: Purple

Occupations: City planning, landscape architecture, interior design

Gems: Sapphires and Jade

Lucky Numbers: 3, 4, 5, 12, 34, 54

Famous Sheep: Jane Austen, Margot Fonteyn, Billie Jean King, Laurence Olivier, Keith Richards, Rudolph Valentino, Lech Walesa

THE MONKEY

Typical Monkeys move quickly through life, tumbling from one intriguing situation to the next, impressing others with their intelligence and wit. Monkeys are sociable, confident, restless, and curious. Monkeys dread routine and thrive on change.

Monkeys are sometimes accused of being manipulative. They laugh at these charges! Can they help it if they're quick on the uptake? They need stimulation. Monkeys in love expect the unexpected and lose interest when love gets too predictable.

ALL ABOUT THE MONKEY

Chinese Name: HOU

Hours of Day: 3:00 P.M. to 4:59 P.M.

Month: August

Natural Friends: Dragons and Rats

Best to Avoid: Tigers

Color: Gold

Occupations: Science, engineering, writing

Gems: Topaz and Aquamarine

Lucky Numbers: 3, 4, 5, 7, 16, 54

Famous Monkeys: Johnny Cash, Ian
   Fleming, Mick Jagger, Bob Marley,
   Martina Navratilova, Diana Ross,
   Elizabeth Taylor

THE ROOSTER

Flamboyant, competitive, and outspoken—these are typical Rooster traits. Self-confidence—and a lack of patience—combine to create a forceful and shrewd personality. High quality is the standard, and they're not afraid to crow about it.

Roosters usually love to strut their stuff, whether at home or on the job. They work hard, play harder, and often exhibit a flashy artistic streak. Roosters like to rule the roost of romance, but once they settle down, it's for keeps.

ALL ABOUT THE ROOSTER

Chinese Name: JI

Hours of Day: 5:00 P.M. to 6:59 P.M.

Month: September

Natural Friends: Oxen and Snakes

Best to Avoid: Rabbits

Color: Peach

Occupations: Performance art, financial consulting, dentistry

Gems: Rubies and Diamonds

Lucky Numbers: 6, 12, 15, 16, 24, 51

Famous Roosters: Eric Clapton, Errol Flynn, Katharine Hepburn, James Mason, Dolly Parton, Richard Wagner

THE DOG

What qualities are most admired in man's best friend? Loyalty, love, and protectiveness. Valued for their devotion, companionship, and attention to the needs of the pack, Dogs are born social and tend to feel completely out of sorts if they're left alone.

But they come with a temper—and both their bark *and* their bite can do damage. Fortunately, such outbursts are rare. They typically occur if the Dog's precious pride is challenged. Otherwise, the Dog remains eternally true-blue, tender, and affectionate.

ALL ABOUT THE DOG

Chinese Name: GOU

Hours of Day: 7:00 P.M. to 8:59 P.M.

Month: October

Natural Friends: Tigers and Horses

Best to Avoid: Dragons

Color: Yellow

Occupations: Religious professions, lawyers, and healing professions

Gems: Jasper and Moonstone

Lucky Numbers: 1, 4, 5, 10, 14, 19

Famous Dogs: David Bowie, Judy Garland, Michael Jackson, Madonna, Sophia Loren, Norman Schwarzkopf, Sylvester Stallone

THE PIG

They do indulge themselves, but they're always ready to extend a helping hand. Pigs are renowned for generosity and a great sense of humor. Typically creative and carefree, they're top-notch organizers too.

Pleasure-loving Pigs expect fulfillment of every whim. They are typically flirtatious and charming, but notoriously private. Pigs are sometimes unbelievably lazy, but they're lovable and easy to forgive. Total trust is essential to their happiness and a sensual romantic life is essential to their well-being.

ALL ABOUT THE PIG

Chinese Name: ZHU

Hours of Day: 9:00 P.M. to 10:59 P.M.

Month: November

Natural Friends: Rabbits and Sheep

Best to Avoid: Snakes

Color: Blue

Occupations: Education, farming, entertainment

Gems: Coral and Beryl

Lucky Numbers: 8, 16, 18, 34, 41, 48

Famous Pigs: Humphrey Bogart, Maria Callas, Jean Harlow, Elton John, Ronald Reagan, Arnold Schwarzenegger, Tennessee Williams

Compatibility Guide

Natural attraction . . . or natural disaster? The potential for fireworks (both good and bad!) between the animal signs is outlined on the following pages. Locate your sign in this compatibility guide, and see what's in store for you and your relationships. A heart (♥) means it's a good match; a cross (✗) means look elsewhere.

	Dog	Dragon	Horse	Monkey	Ox
DOG	♥ page 87	✗ page 76	♥ page 81	♥ page 85	✗ page 66
DRAGON	✗ page 76	♥ page 74	♥ page 74	♥ page 75	✗ page 63
HORSE	♥ page 81	♥ page 74	✗ page 80	✗ page 80	✗ page 64
MONKEY	♥ page 85	♥ page 75	✗ page 80	♥ page 84	♥ page 65
OX	✗ page 66	✗ page 63	✗ page 64	♥ page 65	♥ page 62
PIG	✗ page 87	♥ page 76	✗ page 82	♥ page 85	♥ page 66

Pig	Rabbit	Rat	Rooster	Sheep	Snake	Tiger
✗ *page 87*	♥ *page 73*	♥ *page 62*	✗ *page 86*	♥ *page 83*	✗ *page 79*	♥ *page 69*
♥ *page 76*	✗ *page 70*	✗ *page 59*	♥ *page 76*	✗ *page 75*	♥ *page 74*	✗ *page 67*
✗ *page 82*	✗ *page 71*	✗ *page 60*	♥ *page 81*	♥ *page 80*	✗ *page 77*	♥ *page 68*
♥ *page 85*	✗ *page 72*	♥ *page 61*	✗ *page 84*	♥ *page 82*	✗ *page 78*	✗ *page 69*
♥ *page 66*	♥ *page 63*	✗ *page 58*	♥ *page 65*	✗ *page 64*	♥ *page 64*	✗ *page 63*
✗ *page 87*	✗ *page 73*	♥ *page 62*	♥ *page 86*	♥ *page 84*	✗ *page 79*	♥ *page 70*

	Dog	Dragon	Horse	Monkey	Ox
RABBIT	♥ page 73	✗ page 70	✗ page 71	✗ page 72	♥ page 63
RAT	♥ page 62	✗ page 59	✗ page 60	♥ page 61	✗ page 58
ROOSTER	✗ page 86	♥ page 76	♥ page 81	✗ page 84	♥ page 65
SHEEP	♥ page 83	✗ page 75	♥ page 80	♥ page 82	✗ page 64
SNAKE	✗ page 79	♥ page 74	✗ page 77	✗ page 78	♥ page 64
TIGER	♥ page 69	✗ page 67	♥ page 68	✗ page 69	✗ page 63

Pig	Rabbit	Rat	Rooster	Sheep	Snake	Tiger
✗ page 73	♥ page 70	✗ page 59	✗ page 73	♥ page 72	♥ page 71	♥ page 67
♥ page 62	✗ page 59	♥ page 58	✗ page 61	✗ page 60	♥ page 60	✗ page 58
♥ page 86	✗ page 73	✗ page 61	✗ page 85	✗ page 83	♥ page 78	✗ page 69
♥ page 84	♥ page 72	✗ page 60	✗ page 83	♥ page 82	♥ page 78	✗ page 68
✗ page 79	♥ page 71	♥ page 60	♥ page 78	♥ page 78	✗ page 77	✗ page 67
♥ page 70	♥ page 67	✗ page 58	✗ page 69	✗ page 68	✗ page 67	♥ page 66

RAT AND RAT: While rivalry may cause tension, two Rats can usually handle it. Take the impulsiveness and pure sex appeal of one Rat, double it—and let the fun and games begin!

RAT AND OX: The Rat's free spirit and the Ox's caution don't usually mix—except in the sexual realm, where bliss is not only possible but probable. But expect day-to-day problems.

RAT AND TIGER: The Tiger's strength appeals to the Rat, but they are destined for romantic turf battles. Remember, the Tiger is fiercely independent, while the Rat prefers constant intimacy.

RAT AND RABBIT: The Rat thrives on adventure, but the Rabbit prefers peace and quiet. Consequently, each feels inhibited by the other. This causes conflict . . . and the Rabbit is sure to run.

RAT AND DRAGON: The Rat and the Dragon are both built for passion and adventure. But, unfortunately, not with each other.

RAT AND SNAKE: The Rat is quick and on the lookout for an opportunity; the Snake is meditative and self-contained. This is a classic case of opposites attracting—very well.

RAT AND HORSE: This is not typically a match made in heaven. Basic personality differences are often irreconcilable, and mutual appreciation tends to be the exception rather than the rule.

RAT AND SHEEP: Both the Rat and the Sheep hold themselves back emotionally, so it's difficult for them to make romantic headway. But with perseverance, this match might work.

RAT AND MONKEY: Mutual attraction is typically automatic, and the romantic future looks like a vacation from worries, boredom, and routine. For these two, risk and romance go hand in hand.

RAT AND ROOSTER: Both are charismatic and attractive, but the Rooster plans and the Rat prefers spontaneity. This basic difference creates a feeling of tension that frequently deflates a potential romance.

RAT AND DOG: Many Rats secretly long for stability, and Dogs can provide it. It may take some adjustment, but this union of opposites can lead to romantic harmony.

RAT AND PIG: A match based on a strong attraction and a deep capacity for true friendship. The Rat and the Pig can share both intimacy and wild times.

OX AND OX: If stability and predictability are the goals, then a pair of Oxen is a good romantic bet. They may not even miss the razzle-dazzle end of love.

OX AND TIGER: The ancient Chinese astrologers put a red light, "Proceed with extreme caution" warning on this love-match. Beware! It could be a romantic kamikaze mission!

OX AND RABBIT: Coziness, comfort, and confrontation-free romance—these are the promises of the Ox and Rabbit match. The shared emotional warmth can get deliciously steamy!

OX AND DRAGON: At worst, the Dragon is aggressive and intolerant. The Ox is stubborn and methodical. If these two clash—and they will—hopes for a peaceful resolution are minimal.

OX AND SNAKE: Both are self-contained, sensual, and faithful—which puts them on the same wavelength. The likelihood of romantic happiness is very promising.

OX AND HORSE: The Ox likes hearth and home; the Horse prefers the open road. Tension builds. Both are hard workers, so business is a better bet than romance.

OX AND SHEEP: The Sheep is oversensitive; the Ox grows tired of walking on eggshells. The Ox rarely lumbers off, but the Sheep can drive the Ox away emotionally.

OX AND MONKEY: The crafty, clever Monkey adds a spark of fun; the Ox provides the forward motion and the stability. This match works if both partners keep their romantic focus.

OX AND ROOSTER: This romantic pair has both the flash and the substance to forge a permanent bond. And it keeps getting sexier as time goes on. A relationship jackpot!

OX AND DOG: The Ox dislikes the Dog's periodic temper tantrums. Unless the Ox shows considerable understanding, this match won't work.

OX AND PIG: Sexual attraction goes a long way between the Pig and the Ox—and animal magnetism is strong too. With nurturing, this love could last.

TIGER AND TIGER: Two Tigers? In the same den? It could lead to the occasional catfight, but purring may also abound. The key is equal time in the spotlight.

TIGER AND RABBIT: The passive Rabbit and the dominant Tiger are made for compatibility. Each respects the other and contributes to a sense of harmony.

TIGER AND DRAGON: Neither the Tiger nor the Dragon is willing to yield the spotlight. Not a good match.

TIGER AND SNAKE: The odds are against this romantic match. The cool Snake and the dignified, distant Tiger have little in common. Both prefer to seek partnership elsewhere.

TIGER AND HORSE: Power and passion—these are the shared traits of the Tiger and the Horse. With this much spirit, romance promises to be at the outer limits of wonderful.

TIGER AND SHEEP: These opposites sometimes attract . . . but it usually wears off once the truth is out: The Tiger is too excitable for the fearful Sheep. Emotional entanglements lead to frustration.

TIGER AND MONKEY: How can the Tiger primp and preen with the Monkey somersaulting overhead? It can't. This is just one of many problems that face this not-in-the-stars love match.

TIGER AND ROOSTER: Both want to rule—the Tiger with its presence and the Rooster with its plans. While they may make a beautiful couple, communication and closeness are not likely.

TIGER AND DOG: Passion and loyalty! This is a match made in heaven. Each partner gets the best of the bargain—and the mutual respect grows into a solid commitment.

TIGER AND PIG: Face it—passion is not the only part of love. What the Tiger and the sensible Pig miss in steaminess, they make up for in substance. A sturdy bond.

RABBIT AND RABBIT: Take two peace-loving, mild-mannered, and stylish Rabbits and put them together. What do you get? Happiness. And it may very well last a lifetime.

RABBIT AND DRAGON: Rabbits are natural peacemakers, and Dragons are fire-breathers. This challenging match can work—but it's usually up to the

Rabbit to provide the understanding and diplomacy.

RABBIT AND SNAKE: Rabbits tend to nurture others, and Snakes appreciate it—especially because the sexual chemistry between these two is legendary. This match has satisfaction with a capital *S*.

RABBIT AND HORSE: Despite their somewhat cool facade, Rabbits tend to need tender, loving care. They do not appreciate the Horse's tendency to gallop away from the ties that bind.

RABBIT AND SHEEP: *Sensitive, soft,* and *sweet*—those are the key words for this romantic match. The Rabbit and the Sheep are born to find each other—and live happily ever after.

RABBIT AND MONKEY: The Rabbit rarely appreciates the Monkey's antics and games—and for very good reasons. They frequently lead to heartbreak. Exercise extreme caution—and expect a bumpy road.

RABBIT AND ROOSTER: Rabbits like to hide, while Roosters like to strut their stuff. If these two can even find each other, it's nothing short of a romantic miracle!

RABBIT AND DOG: The Dog's stability lends a happy balance to the Rabbit's moodiness. Rabbits are sentimental, a trait that Dogs love. Both are social— and both sides win in this love match.

RABBIT AND PIG: Both love pleasure, sensual delights, and self-indulgence— but after the passion cools, the relationship will fade.

DRAGON AND DRAGON: Two Dragons are bound to clash, but they can also learn to compromise. Once that skill is mastered, this red-hot team will stay happily on its toes.

DRAGON AND SNAKE: Fiery energy and cool wisdom make this a relationship with natural balance—and passion. And since both are great wits, the loving and the conversation are equally stimulating.

DRAGON AND HORSE: Physical attraction and mental compatibility combine to create an all-around romantic party.

Each must temper a natural impulse: the Dragon's to rule, and the Horse's to run away.

DRAGON AND SHEEP: The Dragon is larger than life; the Sheep tends to hide. It's possible that these two will spot each other across a crowded room . . . but it's unlikely.

DRAGON AND MONKEY: A mutual admiration society is almost inevitable between this complementary couple. It's likely that the admiration will blossom into love—forever.

DRAGON AND ROOSTER: One breathes fire while the other crows. Both want the spotlight—and are reluctant to share. Harmony is tough, but possible—and when it works, it's grand.

DRAGON AND DOG: Both possess a temper—and when the tempers flare up into flames, it's not a pretty sight. The disaster potential is high in this star-crossed romance.

DRAGON AND PIG: The Dragon needs a mellow, tolerant partner, and the Pig thrives on a bit of romantic excitement.

This match sparkles with the possibility of long-term happiness.

SNAKE AND SNAKE: A meeting of the minds is predictable and satisfying, but the jealousy and possessiveness of two intertwined Snakes is likely to present a formidable romantic challenge.

SNAKE AND HORSE: The Snake calmly meditates while the Horse dances and prances. In order for this to work, each must commit to developing an appreciation for the other's disparate lifestyle.

SNAKE AND SHEEP: This is a heavenly love match. The Sheep's compassionate strength impresses the Snake; the Snake's philosophical bent delights the Sheep—a perfect combination of wit, warmth, and wisdom.

SNAKE AND MONKEY: They share sharp intelligence and an abundance of confidence, but the Snake is secretive and the Monkey is too restless to search for soul secrets. This relationship takes work.

SNAKE AND ROOSTER: Snakes focus on the inner world and Roosters on the outer. Together, they can rule the universe! And create a new galaxy for themselves—behind closed doors.

SNAKE AND DOG: Sexual pleasure is likely in this match, but so are problems. Chances of a long-term relationship are slim.

SNAKE AND PIG: The Pig's flirtatiousness ignites the Snake's jealousy—and no amount of meditation eases the tension. This match brings new meaning to the term "conflict." Tread carefully!

HORSE AND HORSE: Two Horses may choose to gallop into romance at high speed, but it may not last for long. Their independent natures ultimately lead to clashes.

HORSE AND SHEEP: The stars are shining full-force on this match. The elegant Horse and the supersensitive Sheep are perfect examples of a blissful union of complementary opposites.

HORSE AND MONKEY: Both dislike routine and demand wild social lives. But when it comes to intimacy, they are perhaps too similar to strike a romantic balance.

HORSE AND ROOSTER: Expect some angry crowing (the Rooster) and some spirited foot-stomping (the Horse). But also expect a thrilling exchange of hearts—with great passion.

HORSE AND DOG: The Horse contributes the glitter, and the Dog provides the stability. This romance has the freedom and security that both crave—and an excellent chance for eternal happiness.

HORSE AND PIG: Because both partners are easygoing, the going is easy but sooner or later, reality asserts itself and each goes off in search of a more responsible mate.

SHEEP AND SHEEP: Both have high ideals, sensitivity, and subtle strength for occasional forays into pure pleasure. Sound like a recipe for romantic fun and games? It is!

SHEEP AND MONKEY: These two perfectly complement (or even compensate for!) each other. What one lacks, the other has. This match often leads to success for both.

SHEEP AND ROOSTER: The Sheep is diplomatic, but the Rooster can push it past all limits. Rooster's cockiness rubs Sheep the wrong way, and neither is likely to want to work it out.

SHEEP AND DOG: Both thrive in an atmosphere of predictable intimacy and both are born to give it. When they pair up, it's a homecoming. And once there, they stay.

SHEEP AND PIG: The good life starts here: coziness, comfort, and pleasure galore! When the Sheep and the Pig find each other, it's the stairway to romantic paradise.

MONKEY AND MONKEY: Birds of a feather flock together, and so do Monkeys. Fun and games, cleverness, and good cheer abound. This is a world-class match.

MONKEY AND ROOSTER: The Monkey tends to take life lightly; the Rooster is picky and unabashedly vocal. It's too much strain on both—and the Monkey usually takes off first.

MONKEY AND DOG: As the Monkey's cleverness perfectly complements the Dog's persistence, this pairing is ideal.

MONKEY AND PIG: Creative and easy-going, the Pig is a good match for the Monkey. They make time for intimate fun, but they may need to be reminded about life's many responsibilities.

ROOSTER AND ROOSTER: There's a reason why cockfights are illegal in so many countries! Be warned: The take-no-prisoners Roosters are better paired with just about anyone else.

ROOSTER AND DOG: There's some tension in this match. The Rooster's ego tends to demand (and then overlook) the Dog's loyalty. Dogs get depressed about this and run away.

ROOSTER AND PIG: The Pig is calm and organized; the Rooster is demanding and shrewd. They may have to work out the details, but the happiness potential is high.

DOG AND DOG: The mutual honesty and devotion are truly intoxicating. The shared trust is exhilarating. This match is as easy as it is romantically fulfilling.

DOG AND PIG: Friendly and affection-ate, this pairing leads to quiet pleasure. But if thrills are required, this is not a particularly promising match.

PIG AND PIG: This relationship starts off hot, but cools when the personality similarities lead to fallout. Enjoy the beginning and prepare for some ups and downs if love continues.

What's Your Chinese Sign?

Jan. 31, 1900 *to* Feb. 18, 1901   Metal Rat

Feb. 19, 1901 *to* Feb. 7, 1902   Metal Ox

Feb. 8, 1902 *to* Jan. 28, 1903   Water Tiger

Jan. 29, 1903 *to* Feb. 15, 1904   Water Rabbit

Feb. 16, 1904 *to* Feb. 3, 1905   Wood Dragon

Feb. 4, 1905 *to* Jan. 24, 1906   Wood Snake

Jan. 25, 1906 *to* Feb. 12, 1907   Fire Horse

Feb. 13, 1907 *to* Feb. 1, 1908   Fire Sheep

Feb. 2, 1908 *to* Jan. 21, 1909   Earth Monkey

Jan. 22, 1909 *to* Feb. 9, 1910   Earth Rooster

Feb. 10, 1910 *to* Jan. 29, 1911   Metal Dog

Jan. 30, 1911 *to* Feb. 17, 1912   Metal Pig

Feb. 18, 1912 *to* Feb. 5, 1913   Water Rat

Feb. 6, 1913	to	Jan. 25, 1914	Water Ox
Jan. 26, 1914	to	Feb. 13, 1915	Wood Tiger
Feb. 14, 1915	to	Feb. 2, 1916	Wood Rabbit
Feb. 3, 1916	to	Jan. 22, 1917	Fire Dragon
Jan. 23, 1917	to	Feb. 10, 1918	Fire Snake
Feb. 11, 1918	to	Jan. 31, 1919	Earth Horse
Feb. 1, 1919	to	Feb. 19, 1920	Earth Sheep
Feb. 20, 1920	to	Feb. 7, 1921	Metal Monkey
Feb. 8, 1921	to	Jan. 27, 1922	Metal Rooster
Jan. 28, 1922	to	Feb. 15, 1923	Water Dog
Feb. 16, 1923	to	Feb. 4, 1924	Water Pig
Feb. 5, 1924	to	Jan. 24, 1925	Wood Rat
Jan. 25, 1925	to	Feb. 12, 1926	Wood Ox
Feb. 13, 1926	to	Feb. 1, 1927	Fire Tiger
Feb. 2, 1927	to	Jan. 22, 1928	Fire Rabbit

Jan. 23, 1928	*to*	Feb. 9, 1929	Earth Dragon
Feb. 10, 1929	*to*	Jan. 29, 1930	Earth Snake
Jan. 30, 1930	*to*	Feb. 16, 1931	Metal Horse
Feb. 17, 1931	*to*	Feb. 5, 1932	Metal Sheep
Feb. 6, 1932	*to*	Jan. 25, 1933	Water Monkey
Jan. 26, 1933	*to*	Feb. 13, 1934	Water Rooster
Feb. 14, 1934	*to*	Feb. 3, 1935	Wood Dog
Feb. 4, 1935	*to*	Jan. 23, 1936	Wood Pig
Jan. 24, 1936	*to*	Feb. 10, 1937	Fire Rat
Feb. 11, 1937	*to*	Jan. 30, 1938	Fire Ox
Jan. 31, 1938	*to*	Feb. 18, 1939	Earth Tiger
Feb. 19, 1939	*to*	Feb. 7, 1940	Earth Rabbit
Feb. 8, 1940	*to*	Jan. 26, 1941	Metal Dragon
Jan. 27, 1941	*to*	Feb. 14, 1942	Metal Snake
Feb. 15, 1942	*to*	Feb. 4, 1943	Water Horse

Feb. 5, 1943	*to*	Jan. 24, 1944	Water Sheep
Jan. 25, 1944	*to*	Feb. 12, 1945	Wood Monkey
Feb. 13, 1945	*to*	Feb. 1, 1946	Wood Rooster
Feb. 2, 1946	*to*	Jan. 21, 1947	Fire Dog
Jan. 22, 1947	*to*	Feb. 9, 1948	Fire Pig
Feb. 10, 1948	*to*	Jan. 28, 1949	Earth Rat
Jan. 29, 1949	*to*	Feb. 16, 1950	Earth Ox
Feb. 17, 1950	*to*	Feb. 5, 1951	Metal Tiger
Feb. 6, 1951	*to*	Jan. 26, 1952	Metal Rabbit
Jan. 27, 1952	*to*	Feb. 13, 1953	Water Dragon
Feb. 14, 1953	*to*	Feb. 2, 1954	Water Snake
Feb. 3, 1954	*to*	Jan. 23, 1955	Wood Horse
Jan. 24, 1955	*to*	Feb. 11, 1956	Wood Sheep
Feb. 12, 1956	*to*	Jan. 30, 1957	Fire Monkey
Jan. 31, 1957	*to*	Feb. 17, 1958	Fire Rooster

Feb. 18, 1958	*to* Feb. 7, 1959	Earth Dog
Feb. 8, 1959	*to* Jan. 27, 1960	Earth Pig
Jan. 28, 1960	*to* Feb. 14, 1961	Metal Rat
Feb. 15, 1961	*to* Feb. 4, 1962	Metal Ox
Feb. 5, 1962	*to* Jan. 24, 1963	Water Tiger
Jan. 25, 1963	*to* Feb. 12, 1964	Water Rabbit
Feb. 13, 1964	*to* Feb. 1, 1965	Wood Dragon
Feb. 2, 1965	*to* Jan. 20, 1966	Wood Snake
Jan. 21, 1966	*to* Feb. 8, 1967	Fire Horse
Feb. 9, 1967	*to* Jan. 29, 1968	Fire Sheep
Jan. 30, 1968	*to* Feb. 16, 1969	Earth Monkey
Feb. 17, 1969	*to* Feb. 5, 1970	Earth Rooster
Feb. 6, 1970	*to* Jan. 26, 1971	Metal Dog
Jan. 27, 1971	*to* Feb. 14, 1972	Metal Pig
Feb. 15, 1972	*to* Feb. 2, 1973	Water Rat

Feb. 3, 1973	to	Jan. 22, 1974	Water Ox
Jan. 23, 1974	to	Feb. 10, 1975	Wood Tiger
Feb. 11, 1975	to	Jan. 30, 1976	Wood Rabbit
Jan. 31, 1976	to	Feb. 17, 1977	Fire Dragon
Feb. 18, 1977	to	Feb. 6, 1978	Fire Snake
Feb. 7, 1978	to	Jan. 27, 1979	Earth Horse
Jan. 28, 1979	to	Feb. 15, 1980	Earth Sheep
Feb. 16, 1980	to	Feb. 4, 1981	Metal Monkey
Feb. 5, 1981	to	Jan. 24, 1982	Metal Rooster
Jan. 25, 1982	to	Feb. 12, 1983	Water Dog
Feb. 13, 1983	to	Feb. 1, 1984	Water Pig
Feb. 2, 1984	to	Feb. 19, 1985	Wood Rat
Feb. 20, 1985	to	Feb. 8, 1986	Wood Ox
Feb. 9, 1986	to	Jan. 28, 1987	Fire Tiger
Jan. 29, 1987	to	Feb. 16, 1988	Fire Rabbit

Feb. 17, 1988	to	Feb. 5, 1989	Earth Dragon
Feb. 6, 1989	to	Jan. 26, 1990	Earth Snake
Jan. 27, 1990	to	Feb. 14, 1991	Metal Horse
Feb. 15, 1991	to	Feb. 3, 1992	Metal Sheep
Feb. 4, 1992	to	Jan. 22, 1993	Water Monkey
Jan. 23, 1993	to	Feb. 9, 1994	Water Rooster
Feb. 10, 1994	to	Jan. 30, 1995	Wood Dog
Jan. 31, 1995	to	Feb. 18, 1996	Wood Pig
Feb. 19, 1996	to	Feb. 6, 1997	Fire Rat
Feb. 7, 1997	to	Jan. 27, 1998	Fire Ox
Jan. 28, 1998	to	Feb. 15, 1999	Earth Tiger
Feb. 16, 1999	to	Feb. 4, 2000	Earth Rabbit
Feb. 5, 2000	to	Jan. 23, 2001	Metal Dragon
Jan. 24, 2001	to	Feb. 11, 2002	Metal Snake
Feb. 12, 2002	to	Jan. 31, 2003	Water Horse
Feb. 1, 2003	to	Jan. 21, 2004	Water Sheep

Jan. 22, 2004	*to* Feb. 8, 2005	Wood Monkey
Feb. 9, 2005	*to* Jan. 28, 2006	Wood Rooster
Jan. 29, 2006	*to* Feb. 17, 2007	Fire Dog
Feb. 18, 2007	*to* Feb. 6, 2008	Fire Pig
Feb. 7, 2008	*to* Jan. 25, 2009	Earth Rat
Jan. 26, 2009	*to* Feb. 13, 2010	Earth Ox
Feb. 14, 2010	*to* Feb. 2, 2011	Metal Tiger
Feb. 3, 2011	*to* Jan. 22, 2012	Metal Rabbit
Jan. 23, 2012	*to* Feb. 9, 2013	Water Dragon
Feb. 10, 2013	*to* Jan. 30, 2014	Water Snake
Jan. 31, 2014	*to* Feb. 18, 2015	Wood Horse
Feb. 19, 2015	*to* Feb. 7, 2016	Wood Sheep
Feb. 8, 2016	*to* Jan. 27, 2017	Fire Monkey
Jan. 28, 2017	*to* Feb. 15, 2018	Fire Rooster
Feb. 16, 2018	*to* Feb. 4, 2019	Earth Dog
Feb. 5, 2019	*to* Feb. 9, 2020	Earth Pig

This book was designed and typeset in Rotis by Ann Obringer of Bedford, New York.